Miscellaneous Pieces

Featuring, The Poetic Flame

A Book of 101 Miscellaneous Poems

by
Robert L. Horton

Copyright © 2017 by Robert L. Horton

ALL RIGHTS RESERVED. No part of this book may be reproduced or transmitted in any form or by any means, including but not limited to, electronic or mechanical, including photocopying, recording, or by any information storage and retrieval system without express written permission from the author.

ISBN: 978-1-946598-01-1

Truth Book Publishers
www.truthbookpublishers.com
truthbookpublishers@yahoo.com

Printed in the United States of America.

For questions or commentary about this book, Robert can be reached at:
damoodypoet@gmail.com

Dedication

For my brother Fred

Forward

My interest in poetry began when I was around 12 years old after I happened across my brother writing a poem. As I recall, some friends and I were outside playing one Saturday morning when we realized that we were short one player. I went inside looking for my brother to join us and found him lying across his bed writing. Excited about him joining us, I asked him to come outside and play teams with us. Without hesitation, he said, "no", I'm writing a poem", and continued writing. I asked him, "What's a poem?" I wasn't actually interested in knowing what a poem was; I was just more intrigued by the fact that he preferred staying inside rather than playing with us. In retrospect, I must admit that Fred was always known to value reading and studying above anything else. Conversely, I was always known to prefer playing. Experiencing my brother choosing to write rather than playing with us always stayed with me.

Three years later, at age 15, I wrote my first poem titled, "A Coming Arrival" (for Deann, my girlfriend then, my wife now). I wrote a poem titled "Trouble", a year later. "Trouble" was an appropriate piece to write because it seemed I was always in it. As a result of always being in trouble, a plethora of poems followed. Over the years, poetry became my outlet as I dealt with the pain of growing up poor, fatherless and from being taken advantage of as a child, which led to a lifetime struggle to find my true identity. I truly thank God for poetry and how writing poems releases me. I have always been a day dreamer, and even now, I constantly find myself in brown-study, visualizing poems I will write. A variety of inspiration led me to write both *Miscellaneous Pieces* and *Released, my first volume.* Those inspirations include: the wonders I see in nature during my daily walk, the lift I get reading the Holy Bible, ideas that evolve through personal conversations, daily news stories, and above all these, my own personal experiences and reactions to life's joys and challenges.

I am truly blessed to have a brother that poured the concrete in which I write poetry upon. As a result, I dedicated *Miscellaneous Pieces* to him. During my childhood and throughout my adult life, I have observed Fred reading, writing, studying and teaching. Observing him spend countless hours perfecting his craft gave me the confidence, courage and inspiration to do the same. Fred, you ignited the poetic flame in me, and I am indebted to you for this. I pray this volume will make you as proud of me as I am of you. I love you brother, you are the greatest! I pray too that you, the reader, will find true inspiration in the pages ahead. In this book you will find a kaleidoscope of topics. I consider it a book that speaks to real life experiences, in real times, for real life people. I hope you enjoy and I thank you for your interest. Peace and God's blessings!

-Robert L. Horton

You know those who want to keep you alive-

They are the ones who speak life into you.
-Robert L. Horton

You know those who want to keep you alive-
They are the ones who speak life into you.

-Robert L. Horton

Table of Contents

Introduction Poem: No Particular Rhyme Or Reason

1.	All That Is Poetic In Life	12
2.	Aspiration	13
3.	An Unfulfilled Life	14
4.	Ali	15
5.	A Renewed Heart	16
6.	Because Of You I Am Me	17
7.	Better With Two	18
8.	Brevity Of Life	19
9.	Belly Fat	20
10.	Blood And Water	21
11.	But What Is God Saying To You?	22
12.	Carry On	23
13.	Confessions Of The Heart	24
14.	Costly Press	25
15.	Casino and Lottery	26
16.	Cost Of Words	27
17.	Dreams And Dreamers Welcomed	28
18.	Deception	29
19.	Day And Night	30
20.	Difference Of Opinion	31
21.	Final Call For A Renewed Life (A Message To Black America)	32
22.	Fearfully And Wonderfully Made (The Saved Black Queen's Perspective)	33
23.	Falsely Accused	34
24.	Flint's Contaminated Water	35
25.	Facebooker Or Real Friend?	36
26.	Flowers Are For The Living	37
27.	Games	38
28.	Guard Your Heart	39
29.	Greed	40
30.	House Slave	41
31.	How You Come Across	42
32.	Hell	43
33.	He Rose Again	44
34.	Isis	45

35.	Jonah	47
36.	Keeping It Off	48
37.	Life And Death (2 Roads)	49
38.	Love And Harmony	50
39.	Looks Don't Tell The Complete Story	51
40.	Life's Paradox And The Ticking Clock	52
41.	Legacy Of Failure	53
42.	Life's Journey	54
43.	My Daily Creed	55
44.	Meals Without Meat	56
45.	My Final Goodbye	57
46.	Nuggets	58
47.	Non-Stoppers	59
48.	Natural Hair	60
49.	Overcoming Your Past	61
50.	On Earth (As It Is Not In Heaven)	62
51.	Press On	63
52.	Pyramids Beyond The Sky	64
53.	Poetry And Me	65
54.	Pass The Torch	66
55.	Praise	67
56.	Quotes	69
57.	Religion Or The Lord's Church?	70
58.	Redemption	71
59.	Sink Or Swim	72
60.	Set Adrift	73
61.	Self-Reflection (A Look Inside)	74
62.	Serenity	75
63.	10 Timely Truths And 10 Spiritual Truths	76
64.	The Poetic Flame	77
65.	The Poetic Zone	78
66.	The Eagles Plight	79
67.	The Same Sun And Moon	80
68.	The Truth Revealed	81
69.	The Bread Of Life	82
70.	The Second Verse	83
71.	The Earth Remains	84
72.	The Matrix	85
73.	Today And Tomorrow	86
74.	The Power Of Love	87
75.	The Procrastinator	88

76.	The Limelight	89
77.	The Cross	90
78.	The Reckoning	91
79.	Thick Skin	92
80.	Trapped	93
81.	Thug Life To Superman	94
82.	The Grind, Competition And Success	95
83.	The Answer Is Me	96
84.	The Right Voice	97
85.	What's The Point?	98
86.	Why I Left	99
87.	When Poets Cry And What Is God To Me?	100
88.	Work While It's Day	101
89.	When Your Story Ends	102
90.	Why?	103
91.	Who's Coming Behind You?	104
92.	Wisdom	105
93.	Wordplay	106
94.	Wait'n On Money	107
95.	When I Go	108
96.	Walking In My Destiny	109
97.	What Color Is Your Water?	110
98.	Your Cross	111
99.	Yesterday	112
100.	Your Success	113
101.	Zealot	114

Bonus Poems:

The Proliferation of Mass Communication/Give And Create/Odyssey/The Long Walk Home/The Poetic Call

No Particular Rhyme Or Reason

There's no particular rhyme or reason,

It's just the season for this book.

So take a look inside-

And you just might be surprised.

Never judge a book or person by their outward cover-

Take it from me, there's more to discover.

Each piece has a different interpretation,

Conjured from my exhaustive imagination-

Written to provide a source of inspiration,

And to empower the next generation.

Sometimes the shortest lines have the greatest impact,

You can be small, but still stand tall, as a matter of fact.

When gifts are expressed, it validates your passion,

And when others are blessed, it brings total satisfaction.

This book is likened to an umbrella in inclement weather,

Your job is to find the remaining pieces and put them all together.

All That Is Poetic In Life   1.

The sun and the moon,
The flowers in bloom-
The oceans and seas,
The changing colors of leaves.

The stars in the constellation,
The bee's act of pollination-
The gentle breeze on a summer's night,
The tiger's stripes and eagles in flight.

The morning dew and winter flakes,
The marriage proposal and wedding cake-
The bride's gown and groom's tux,
The king's crown and peacock's strut.

The majestic mountains and artist brush,
The magnificent rainbow and intimate touch-
The baby's smile and cherubic face,
The poets pen and God's grace.

"God and His creation is poetry in motion."

Aspiration 2.

I aspire to do what's right.
To live up to the things I write-
How about you?
I had to grow to reach my current height-
Becoming a better man is what I'm striving to do.

"Singers, artist and poets write, sing and perform some of the most awe inspiring things. But sometimes our behavior doesn't always compliment what we sing or write about. Forgive us of our shortcomings as we aspire to become better people. Because the messages we convey in our art form goes for us first. And only after we receive our own messages, do we then have permission to share with the world."

An Unfulfilled Life   3.

What did you dedicate your life too?
What did you live for?
Did all your dreams come true?
Or did you live unfulfilled wanting more?

Did you share when you had it to give?
Did you help others in their time of need?
Were you an example on how to live?
Or did you worship the god of greed?

Did you love and let your light shine?
Did you strive to do your best?
Did you learn to respect the value of T.I.M.E?
Or did you fail when challenged by a test?

Did you take life serious enough?
Did you push past your pain?
Did you overcome when times got tough?
Or was life to you just a game?

"**Life is God's gift to you. And He has placed many talents within you.
But don't die with what He gave you, die empty.**"

Ali   4.

"The ultimate measure of a man is not where he stands in moments of comfort and convenience, but where he stands in times of challenge and controversy."
-Dr. King

God made him fast,
Faster than eyes can see-
He floated like a butterfly and stung like a bee.
Born Cassious Clay-
But died Muhammad Ali.
Black manhood is his legacy to me-
To the greatest of all time, R.I.P.

"In the ring you showed and proved what you could do. Outside the ring you stood strong when it mattered most. Against all odds you risked it all for what you believed. You shook up the world with your courageous stand and we can still feel the vibration. There will never be another like you. Rest In Peace Champ."

A Renewed Heart 5.

The peace of God is a real gift,
That the world can't give you-
Depraved hearts need a lift,
And must be made anew.

To renew your heart is His delight,
To give you a heart of flesh-
Your heart must first be contrite,
And all sin must be confessed.

The Lord Speaks:

"I, The Lord search the heart,
I also try the reins-
To reveal what's hidden in the dark,
Exposing those serving me in vain.

Man's heart remains depraved,
Without the renewing of his mind-
Return to me and be saved,
Mankind is running out of time."

"Behold, I stand at the door and knock. If anyone hears my voice and opens his heart, I will come in to him and eat with him and he with me."
Revelation 3:20

Because Of You, I Am Me   **6.**

Because of you, I Am me.
You blazed the trail-
You paved the way.
Because of you, I cannot fail-
Because of you, I'm here today.
Ancestral roots justifies a mighty tree-
Because of you, I Am me.

"Once their sacrifice was made the path was laid.
Our ancestors became the light so we could see."

Better With Two   7.

One can be fun,
But it's better with two-
Basking in the sun,
Looking over at you.

With you I feel complete,
You're the shadow of my soul-
You epitomize a help meet,
Together we'll grow old.

We've had our share of pain,
But we made it through-
There's sunshine after the rain,
Truly blessed by having you.

You bring out the best in me,
I owe you my life-
You are my destiny,
Honored having you as my wife.

"For my wife and best friend Deann, who truly personifies a help meet."

Brevity Of Life

We must leave this place,
It's no longer safe here-
But dreams deferred is a disgrace,
Don't be paralyzed by fear.

Life is just too short,
To be giving up hope-
Life is a T.E.A.M sport,
Especially when difficult to cope.

God made the world good,
Even though you see bad-
Govern yourself as you should,
And make your soul glad.

This world will pass away,
No more evil and sin-
Anticipating that glorious day,
For God's kingdom to begin!

"Occupy till I come."
Luke 19:13

Belly Fat 9.
My belly fat kept getting in the way, so I had to get rid of it.

I served notice on my belly fat today,
My fat assumed that it was here to stay-
It was time for change, because I'd had enough,
So I took control and got off my butt!

But when I lose weight I find it again,
My belly fat returns like a long lost friend-
But my new goal is to be healthy and lean,
Now I follow a vegan diet and workout routine.

I found my voice when I lost my weight,
I reached my goal and now I feel great-
With each passing day my confidence grows,
And now with ease I can touch my toes.

Prayerfully my belly fat is gone for good,
I'm committed to doing what I know I should-
My decree to keeping it off this time,
Stopping and starting is a harder hill to climb.

"What's not needed shouldn't exist."

Blood And Water   10.

They say blood is thicker,
But water flows quicker-
We need both to survive,
Both flowed when Christ died.

Jesus Christ is the savior of men,
His shed blood was atonement for sin-
Water won't quench man's spiritual thirst,
Christ was slain before the foundations of the earth.

"**Life is in the blood and water.**"

But What Is God Saying To You?   11.

You have complete clarity when it comes to me,
Even though you're in bondage and I am free-
You know exactly what I'm supposed to do,
But what is God saying to you?

When you judge me, you condemn yourself,
Money isn't as valuable as spiritual wealth-
What you tell me must go for you too-
But what is God saying to you?

Sermons you hear are for you to receive,
Letting your light shine causes others to believe-
Humility allows Gods love to flow through,
But what is God saying to you?

Let those without sin cast the first stone,
The one qualified to judge sits on His throne-
The Holy Spirit affirms what I'm saying is true,
But what is God saying to you?

"It behooves you to pay attention to what The Father is saying to you."

Carry On   **12.**

There's so much to do,
With little time to do it-
Sometimes life can overwhelm you,
And make you want to quit.

But you gotta be strong,
Because you have to share-
Let your motto be: **_To Carry On,_**
And spend time in prayer.

There's so much to do,
With little time to do it-
Sometimes life can overwhelm you,
And make you want to quit.

But you gotta be strong,
Because you have to share-
Let your motto be: **_To Carry On,_**
And spend time in prayer.

"Today demands your strength."

Confessions Of The Heart

Lord, you and I are going to meet later, so we might as well talk now.

I confessed to God what my sins are,

He replied, "Son you were created to shine like a star.

And although you fell short sometimes,

I decreed that you will always be mine.

I graced you when you got off track,

Your soul was compromised after coming under attack.

And then you believed Satan's lies,

But I counted all the tears you cried.

And my grace is sufficient for you,

Every storm you encountered I carried you through.

To your divine calling always stay true-

Sharing your poetic gift you must faithfully do."

"Yes Lord. And so it shall be."

Costly Press   **14.**

Why is everything I say news?
Is it because you profit off my views?
Criticizing me, but couldn't walk a mile in my shoes,
Haters are nothing but cowards who haven't paid dues.

"Constructive criticism is better than constant scrutiny."

Casino   15.

They go in with big dreams,
And try their luck at casino machines-
With hopes of getting rich they pull the lever,
But don't come out any better.

Lottery

I Am a son,
My Father is a king-
When my change comes,
Riches it will bring.

I've been waiting a long time,
And it'll be worth the wait-
This year I'll receive what's rightfully mine,
Winning the lotto is my fate!

There's so much I want to do,
Make a difference and visit exotic places-
Being rich will be a dream come true,
Living the good life and putting smiles on little faces.

What's for me I shall receive,
I always knew I would win-
Good things come to those who believe,
And next year I'll win it again.

"**Play responsibly.**"

Cost Of Words

The air we breathe is free, but words cost,
Once they're released, you're not the boss.

Don't say things that you'll later regret,
Don't let loose lips write a bad check.

Treat others with dignity and respect,
Hurtful words have such a negative effect.

So before saying something mean, think twice-
Say something nice, or risk paying an awful price.

"Death and life are in the power of the tongue."
Proverbs 18:21

Dreams   17.
Dreams make a higher reality possible.

Life was inspired by a dream,
Dreams introduce you to a new reality-
But in order to interpret what they mean,
You must go beyond where eyes can't see.

Dreams converse between Heaven and earth,
And give insight into the world of divine-
Dreams become reality by proving your worth,
Dreams also refresh and develop the mind.

Dreams reveal hidden thoughts then flee the scene,
But you must recapture them when you awake-
Dreams are taken for granted out of routine,
Lost messages from Heaven can be a costly mistake.

Dreams are magical moments for you to keep,
Dreams help to guide you along the way-
Dreams occur during the R.E.M. stage of sleep,
Dreams provide hope and inspiration for the next day.

"God speaks in dreams and visions of the night."
Job 33:15-16

Dreamers Welcomed

To dream and create-
To envision a meal on an empty plate.
To build a rhyme from a blank slate-
To expect love on a blind date.
Dreams are creative energy-
Sent to inspire you and me.

"Be a dreamer."

Deception 18.
Self-deception is the worse deception.

Deception starts in the heart,
Then corrupts the mind-
Sin runs amuk in the dark,
And death becomes a matter of T.I.M.E.

So please don't be deceived,
By the enemy's crafty ways-
Freedom is a gift for those who believe,
But sin keeps you a slave.

"Be not deceived, God is not mocked. For whatsoever a man soweth, that shall he also reap."
Galatians 6:7

Day And Night

Day is the shadow of night,
Wrong is the opposite of right-
Wisdom guides the eagles in flight,
Eyes are prerequisites to sight.

God is the author of love,
Blessings come from up above-
Peace is represented by a dove,
Rainbows prove the earth won't flood.

Night is the shadow of day,
Burdens are lifted when you pray-
We are vessels made of clay,
Christ is the light, truth and way.

Jesus paid the price for sin-
There's no condemnation being in Him,
His mercy and grace will never end-
You'll never find a better friend.

"I have made a covenant with day and night that they will always come at their proper time."
Jeremiah 33:20

Difference Of Opinion   20.

Listening to me doesn't mean you agree-
But it's rude to cut off.
Mutual respect is always the key-
Allow me to get my point across.

Because if you pause and hear my side-
Our difference of opinion won't collide.
Then after our conversation dies-
We can keep it moving in stride.

"It's O.K to agree to disagree brothers and sisters but let's find common ground and build from there."

Final Call For A Renewed Life 21.
(A Message To Black America)

To get through life you need daily inspiration,
Sharing the Gospel of Christ is our Christian obligation-
The wayward soul needs a spiritual revival,
Restoration begins by reading The Holy Bible.

The cares of this world will choke out life,
Peace will increase when we cease from strife-
To secure our future we need to get along,
Not being each other's keeper is how we went wrong.

We can't turn back the hands of time,
Repentance will halt further spiritual decline-
Love transcends hate when you change your view,
Lifting each other is what we now must do.

The power to heal comes from within,
We can't be God's chosen and full of sin-
Freedom requires unity and working together,
This Is The Final Call For Us To Do Better.

"The T.I.M.E is nigh for us to come together as a people and work together for our collective good."

Fearfully And Wonderfully Made 22.
(The Saved Black Queen's Perspective)

I thank God for my eyes so I can see,
All the other gifts that He bestowed upon me.
Like my ears, nose and lips-
Along with my kinky hair and sway of my hips.
I thank The Most High for my backside too,
You look at it and surmise what it can do for you.
Yes, I am fearfully and wonderfully made-
But this Black Queen will not be played.

And whoever gets this won't hit it and quit it,
But only a God fearing man will understand this.
And before I open my soul to you-
You will put a ring on it and say I do.
I Am on a higher spiritual level,
Because God is my father and not the devil.
And I won't be mistreated or defeated,
So all that flattering talk you can keep it.
Yes, I can be sexy and still be saved-
Because this Black Queen is fearfully and wonderfully made.

"Black women you are the Supreme Queens of the universe.
Never give your power away to an unequal who isn't worthy or deserving of you."

Falsely Accused   **23.**

When laughter turns it burns inside,
You believe the hype from what others write-
You have concerned eyes from digesting lies,
But for my namesake I'm willing to fight.

I was doing just fine before making headlines,
But you never know where life might find you-
Without faith in God I would've lost my mind,
But giving up is something I could never do.

It's hard to have joy when you're falsely accused,
No one wants their name dragged through the mud-
You go and bless others but leave feeling used,
But you must disavow hate and still show love.

A good name is more desired than great wealth,
Being esteemed before men goes a long way-
Fame won't be at the expense of spiritual health,
Regardless of what any of my enemies write or say.

"When the time arrives for you to defend yourself The Holy spirit will give you what to say."
Luke 12:12

Flint's Contaminated Water   24.

Flint's contaminated water,
Infected my beautiful daughter.
She went in to take a bath-
And came out with a rash.
She also broke out in hives,
Poisoned water in our community is destroying innocent lives!
But in America how could this be?
We languish at the bottom rung of a racist society.
So here is my plea to the powers that be,
Fix our water supply-
Before more of our children get sick or die.

"A preventable crisis that is totally unacceptable to the people of Flint.
We demand better from our elected officials!"

Facebooker Or Real Friend?

Are you a Facebooker or real friend?
Because real friends will spend money-
On your support can I depend?
Talk with no action will never be funny.

Your kind post don't reflect your behavior,
You're always so concerned whenever we greet-
But you never respond to any fundraiser,
A donation from you is like pulling teeth.

Are your constant post just empty talk,
Do your dollars back up what you say-
Don't just post on-line but walk the walk,
Issues that matter don't just go away.

Are you a Facebooker or real friend?
Because real friends will spend money-
On your support can I depend?
Talk with no action will never be funny.

"Let us do a better job at supporting our "*Friends.*"

Flowers Are For The Living   26.

This world will honor you,
But you must die first-
But why wait when respect is due,
Why should accolades follow a hearse?

Flowers are for the living,
Don't wait till they pass away-
Celebrate others by sacrificial giving,
Show love and appreciation each day.

We are seeds that will soon be planted,
Because T.I.M.E is the enemy of mankind-
Yet, we still take so much for granted,
But daily we are running out of T.I.M.E.

May this be a wake-up call,
To give each other our best-
Today I pledge to give my all,
Then in peace I'll be laid to rest.

"Flowers are an expression of life and a sign of love that the living should enjoy."

Games   **27.**

The childish games that men play,
Eventually come to an end-
On judgement day what will you say,
You'll learn not to play them again.

Unaware of what's coming down the pike,
But when judgement comes it's too late-
That's why it pays to do what's right,
Playing childish games could seal your fate.

But I used to play games too,
This hard truth I must confess-
Playing games is all I used to do,
But childish games brings unnecessary stress.

Games are for kids, not for grown men,
Just keep it real and stop the charade-
Games that men play always lead to sin,
Eventually, you'll be the one that gets played.

"Are you done playing too?"

Guard Your Heart   28.

Do you love your heart?
Then never take a bribe,
Beware of offers after dark-
And the deceitfulness of pride.

"Out of the heart flow the issues of life."
Proverbs 4:23

Greed

I really hate being overweight,
But I don't know where to begin-
I constantly dream about being in shape,
I'm so ashamed because greed is a sin.

When food calls I'm by the phone,
Because this big girl loves to eat-
To indulge is why I rush to get home,
Belly so big I can't see my feet.

I gotta get to an exercise class,
God knows I regret getting this big-
I get depressed looking at my hips and ass,
I'm as wide as my Frigidaire fridge.

I learned the importance of walking again,
Now I count calories before I eat-
Prayer helped me to exercise discipline,
And my esteem is growing each day of the week!

"Diet and regular exercise are key ingredients to sustained weight loss."

House Slave   30.
(For the fearful who question their abilities)

Hey you.

Yeah you.

You who are reading this piece-

You also got something that needs released.

Because you got something to prove too-

To thine own self, always be true.

Don't be a tamed house slave,

Instead, be brave and runaway-

And perfect thy gift along the way.

"It's T.I.M.E. Let's go. Catch up. You can make it."

How You Come Across   31.

How you come across,
Will not get you far-
Today you're the boss,
Tomorrow a fallen star.

Everyone can't handle power,
It goes straight to their head-
The company's morale is sour,
Demeaning others to stay ahead.

You were once where I'm at,
But forgot where you came from-
Employees are not doormats,
You messed with the wrong one.

The money I made, I saved,
This job I won't miss-
I'll start a business to get paid,
Because today I quit!

"Do unto others as you would have them do unto you."
Luke 6:31

Hell

When he died he carried nothing away,
While living he gratified every fleshy desire-
When he opened his eyes it was judgment day,
And was cast into the lake of burning fire.

There was no relief from his agony and pain,
During his life he didn't believe Hell was real-
Seeking respite from the fire he prays for rain,
Begging God for another chance to do His will.

He wanted to return home and warn his brothers,
Hoping to keep them from the same fate-
He weeps from the haunting words of his mother,
But is forever condemned because now it's too late.

Hell is where Satan will eventually reside,
Hell is eternal punishment for rejecting the truth-
Hell was created for Satan's rebellion and pride,
You can repent and believe or die and have proof.

"And whosoever was not found written in the book of life was cast into the lake of fire."
Revelation 20:15

He Rose Again   33.

Jesus is love,
And His love was expressed-
By shedding His blood,
And sin was addressed.

He sacrificed His life,
While we were in sin-
His death was the price,
Then He rose again.

Why hast thou forsaken me,
Spoken with His last breath-
Only God can set free,
And has power over death.

If I be lifted up,
I will draw all men-
I drank from my Father's cup,
Then I rose again.

"The son of man will be given over to be crucified but on the third day will rise again."
Luke 24:7

Isis 34.

They're here to incite fear-
Because the end times are here,
Murder and mayhem is in their heart-
The demonic beast is placing his mark.

Wicked men on assignment from hell-
The rider is death and the horse is pale,
They lust for power and are equipped for war-
Days like these we haven't seen before.

Isis has cells throughout the nation-
Using brutal attacks for world domination,
Their hearts are dark and devoid of love-
The moon will soon be covered in blood.

But didn't you hear the trumpet sound?
The Angels of death are all around,
Isis isn't leaving but is here to stay-
The last sign before judgement day.

"The last days are upon us. Jesus is soon to return."

Jonah

I didn't give you someone else's stuff,
I gave you what I had-
But according to you it wasn't enough,
So you left disappointed and mad.

But I wish you all the best,
Because I've been where you're at-
For the disobedient, there is no rest,
I'll be here when you get back.

Tough times bring out the worst in some,
You have ears, but refuse to listen-
From your problems you can't outrun,
Your relationship with God is what's missing.

Return like the prodigal son did,
God has open arms waiting for you-
There's a better life for you to live,
To fulfill the purpose He called you to do.

"Wherever you go your problems follow. Whatever you're running from will eventually catch up to you and overtake you. Stop running. Confront and conqueror."

Keeping It Off 36.

You got in shape,
Lost a lot of weight-
Was in a better mental state,
And felt absolutely great!

But you got off track,
Gained twice as much back-
Now upset and calling yourself fat,
And your self-esteem is under attack.

So now you're stuck,
In a depressed rut-
Contemplating giving up,
Complaining, while sitting on your butt.

But change your negative attitude,
And put on your walking shoes-
And begin again paying dues,
Because you got weight to lose.

Start taking steps of faith,
Walk until you lose the weight-
Because it's never too late-
To get back in shape.

And this time you'll win,
By remembering you're the boss-
And when you lose it again,
This time you'll keep it off.

"It will be different this time. This time you will lose and maintain in Jesus name."

Life And Death (2 Roads)   37.

The wide road is full of sin,
It twists and turns then comes to a dead end-
The narrow road leads to eternal life,
And is illuminated by the precious blood of Christ.

Sin blinds and keeps you in the dark,
Then you can't tell the two roads apart-
The wrong road leads further from the light,
Like lost sheep who've wandered out of sight.

The Bible is our guide on how to live,
God's gift of salvation is His pleasure to give-
On Calvary's Cross Jesus took our sins away,
His life was the price He had to pay.

Dying without Christ is another soul lost,
Jesus is our Good Shepherd because He paid the cost-
So choose the road to life made anew,
Eternity with Christ is God's desire for you.

"Enter through the narrow gate."
Matthew 7:13

Love And Harmony   **38.**

I love my life,
Because God gave it to me-
It helps having a supportive wife,
Working together in harmony.

But some travel this road alone,
Without experiencing a soul mate-
Some have regrets when there's drama at home,
Singleness is good when it's worth the wait.

Two can't walk together unless they agree,
Because opposites don't always attract-
For healthy relationships, forgiveness is key,
So think it through before you act.

It takes work to become one flesh,
When the ring goes on it's time to do-
Strive daily to give each other your best,
God will see your efforts and bless you.

"A man who findeth a wife finds a good thing and obtains favor from The Lord."
Proverbs 18:22

Looks Don't Tell The Complete Story   39.

I don't have a clue-
About the story behind you.
And neither can you see-
The story behind me.

So try not to stare-
And approach me with care.
Why judge from such a limited view?
Looks don't tell the complete story of what people have been through.

But take it from me-
There's more to the story than what your eyes can see.
So keep the focus where it needs to be-
On you and not me.

"Judge not."
Matthew 7:1

Life's Paradox And The Ticking Clock   40.

The blind want to see,
The deaf want to hear-
Slaves want to be free,
Distance wants to be near.

Your potential to be great,
Is God's gift to you-
Choices you make determine your fate,
Love yourself and remain true.

Only opened eyes can see,
Only listening ears can hear-
Break the chains to be free,
Come close to be near.

T.I.M.E is limited on earth,
So do all you can-
Always value your self-worth,
And trust in God's plan.

**"Use what God has given to you to the best of your ability.
Be grateful for every blessing and use your time wisely."**

Legacy Of Failure

He thought he would fail,
So he never would try-
They said he was dumb,
And he believed the lie.

And the words he spoke,
Were always so negative-
And the legacy of failure,
He passed down to his kids.

"For as a man thinketh in his heart, so is he."
Proverbs 23:7

Life's Journey 42.

Hearts don't beat long enough,
And the mind can never sleep-
Life's journey is often rough,
The pain from valleys run deep.

Lust and pride are evil twins,
Believers are God's chosen people-
Death is the penalty for sin,
But salvation is God's sequel.

Be consumed with doing right,
Don't give wrong a chance-
Daily walk toward the light,
So God's will can advance.

Learn what you need to know-
The seed of life you have to sow.
With the right information you can grow-
Get it right before you go.

"There are no do-overs in life and we are only here for a little while. Each day is another opportunity to become a better person. So let's get better, do better and be better."

My Daily Creed   43.

Today will be a blessed day-
I rebuke all negativity coming my way.
I'll wear a smile and I won't complain-
And tomorrow will be the same in Jesus name!

"Speak your blessed day into existence."

Meals Without Meat

Welcome to Meals Without Meat,
Thank you, we'd like a table for two-
Certainly, just follow me to your seat,
My name is Tara and I'll be serving you.

Everything looks so delicious my dear,
And the meals are an affordable price-
Thank you honey for bringing me here,
This holistic restaurant is very nice.

Are you ready to order yet sir or mam?
Yes, I'll have the lettuce wrap with spaghetti-
And I'll take the stuffed tomato with candy yams,
Certainly, and I'll return when your order is ready.

Did you two enjoy your meal?
We did, and look forward to coming again-
My pleasure serving you, here is your bill,
And I'll see you two next time my friends.

"We need restaurants like this in our community."

My Final Goodbye

When my life is gone, so am I,
All born of women are destined to die-
But while living I overcame the devils lie,
This poem serves as my final goodbye.

We are vessels for gifts to flow through,
But before gifts flow, they must reach you-
Some just roam and don't have a clue,
Many are called, but the chosen are few.

Walk in your purpose under the sun,
Show how life is supposed to be done-
Nine lives is a myth, you only get one,
Receive The Lord as He bids you to come.

Always give thanks and keep God first,
Live your life for all that its worth-
I've dreamed of Heaven since the day of my birth,
Now I reside, no longer a guest on earth.

"Feels good to be home."

Nuggets

Laugh now because tears are coming,
What you don't see, go and create-
If you can't fight, take off running,
Choices you make determine your fate.

Blend in or stand out,
Because you can't do both-
Without faith you'll be full of doubt,
What you do best, you do most.

What looks good could be bad for you,
Just ask Adam and Eve-
They discovered only God's word is true,
Sin deceives and makes you hide and grieve.

When you're humbled, you serve people,
You never know where life will find you-
So treat everyone as an equal,
Grace performed what the law couldn't do.

"Food for thought."

Non-Stoppers   47.

You know who they are.
You see them coming a mile away.
People looking for you to fail.
Information Seekers.
But not seeking information to better themselves,
Or to help you further your dreams-
But seeking for the purpose of stopping you.

They think you don't know who they are.
They smile and pretend like they're on your team-
But are secretly envious of you and desire to be in your shoes.
And since they're not-
Their only mission is to bring you down.
But you see them for who they are-
Non-Stoppers, and keep it moving.

"Get thee behind me Satan and all those you send my way. Because God is my Father and He is with me and you won't stop me."

Natural Hair

Sista's do you care,
To wear your natural hair-
Or is it too thick for you,
And you can't get a pick through.

But say it loud, "I'm natural and I'm proud!"
Don't let natural hair get lost in the crowd-
Natural hair compliments your hue,
And is God's gift to you.

While true beauty lies within,
Love your hair and color of your skin-
Many parts make up the whole,
Heavenly attributes make you a beautiful soul.

No other hair compares to yours,
Fake hair Black Queens of Africa never wore-
Your power and beauty shapes the world,
Afro's, braids, waves, locs or tight springy curls.

"Perfect beauty is natural beauty."

Overcoming Your Past   **49.**

You must move with life,
Or it just passes you by-
A discontent soul is full of strife,
And you just wanna die.

Being happy is not easy to do,
Especially with so many haters lurking-
Your past is brought up to embarrass you,
They're digging up dirt while you're busy working.

Those who judge me are not mistake free,
Sometimes the greatest teacher is the ground-
I'm still striving to become a better me,
Those who do the least make the loudest sounds.

No weapon formed shall prosper against me,
The Father has more for me to do-
And by His grace I'll reach my destiny,
So I keep the faith and remain true.

"Overcome and keep coming."

On Earth (As It Is Not In Heaven) 50.

On earth there is all manner of evil and sin,
Like the killing of unarmed Black women, children and men.

On earth there is immeasurable suffering, heartache and pain,
From tornados, fires and flooding from all the rain.

On earth there is destruction from war, genocide and rape,
And criminals whose savagery is fueled by hate.

On earth children are sex slaves being bought and sold,
But in Heaven there is peace and streets paved with gold!

"In this world you will have trouble.
But be of good cheer because I have overcome the world."
John 16:33

Press On   51.

Release the beast and the rage within,
Festering hate in your heart is a sin-
You must learn to forgive in order to live,
Life has more to offer and you have more to give.

Trials and tribulations aren't unique to you,
Whatever comes your way you can make it through-
Others have suffered more and gone much farther,
Your attitude and response is what makes life harder.

Life wasn't promised to be a smooth ride,
But God won't forget all the tears you've cried-
Oftentimes life can be difficult to cope,
But continue to believe and never lose hope.

The resurrection proves new life will come,
Keep Pressing On Because Your Work Is Not Done-
Trust in the Lord and keep the faith,
And be exceedingly glad because thy reward is great!

"Press on toward the high mark for the prize of the high calling which is in Christ Jesus."
Philippians 3 14:15

Pyramids Beyond The Sky

I know where saints go after they die,
To the **City of Pyramids** beyond the sky-
Pyramids on earth reflect our Heavenly home,
Pharaohs reflect God's kingship on the throne.

Their steeple chase affirm the messiah's ascension,
Their strategic location reflects the earth's dimensions-
Entombed remains prepared them for another life,
And foreshadowed the resurrection of Jesus Christ.

One of the seven wonders of the earth,
And where Christ was hidden after His birth-
God knew His enemies wouldn't find him there,
He learned about the future cross He would bear.

Pyramids truly are a Heavenly design,
Revealed by God during the conversation before time-
Then erected by the hands of African men,
And the secret to re-building them lies within.

"His kingdom is our eternal home."

Poetry And Me

Inspired poetic messages dance across my mind,
And every message that I receive, rhymes.

With spiritual insight I'm compelled to write,
And sometimes this process takes all night.

And when writing poems becomes a chore,
I look up and say, **"I ain't writing no more"**
But inspired messages are hard to ignore.

"The burden and passion of poetry."

Pass The Torch   54.

Pass the torch of inspiration,
And ignite someone else-
Influence the next generation,
And give more of yourself.

Like Ali, shake up the earth,
In God's image to be great-
With boldness prove your self-worth,
Because excellence is your fate.

There's much to be done-
So let your light shine-
Like Christ the anointed one,
Only sight can lead the blind.

Have the courage to care,
Lift your neighbor in need-
When called upon be there,
And always follow God's lead.

"You are blessed to be a blessing."

Praise   55.

Calm the storm with your praise,
Because the devil's in the air-
Curious souls stop and stare,
And unbelievers will be saved.

Nations gather to worship the King,
Glory and honor belong to Christ-
The one who gave up His life,
He is risen is why we sing!

Lord we lift up your name,
No one else compares to you-
And thy Holy Word is true,
You change not, but remain the same.

Calm the storm with your praise,
Because the devils in the air-
Curious souls stop and stare,
And unbelievers will be saved.

"We were created to give Him the praise."

Quotes

"If you could do it you wouldn't have to talk about it. It would already be done and speaking for itself."

"From coast to coast humanity is in the same boat.
All need love and hope to stay afloat-
Without it, we'll sink together.

"'I'm paying for my past and saving for my future."

"Those learning from their mistakes are in the process of becoming great."

"I expect greatness out of you."
(Spoken to me by my daughter Amaiya as I left for work).

"When you need someone to talk too, listen to your inner voice."

"Spreaders of gossip are in no hurry to spread it when it's about them."

"I wasn't compelled to write until I learned how to read."

"Healed and forgiven is how I'm living."

"Don't spend too much time talking about your successes or failures-
  Instead, put it in a book for others to discover."
_____

"If I add any meaning or value to the world, it will come from something I write."
_____

"There's a time to trust others and a time to trust yourself."
_____

"There are no barriers in life, just hurdles and walls of opportunity."
_____

Religion Or The Lord's Church?   57.

I didn't come to get hurt,
I came to get healed-
I'm still looking for The Lord's Church,
And a pastor who's keeping it real.

These are times of social unrest,
People everywhere are on the edge-
They are losing hope from all the stress,
One step from going over the ledge.

We need relevant churches in this hour,
Not hypocritical judgment zones-
I left when I didn't feel God's power,
So I choose to worship at home.

We need to build up one another,
To prevent more souls from being lost-
Can you love God and hate your brother,
Better examples will lead sinners to the cross.

"To the countless churches across the world who are doing the work of The Lord, I implore you to keep up the great work. Your invaluable service is needed more than ever in this hour. This piece is in no way intended to be an indictment on all churches."

Redemption   **58.**
For Luis Monroy

My boss said this while sitting at his desk,
His God inspired words I will never forget-
**"It's redemption, everyone deserves a second chance,
At this company you can grow and advance."**

Hearing his words were a blessing to me,
They inspired new hope and set me free-
Every day at work I give it my best,
A hundred and ten percent, not one percent less.

It feels so good to be working again,
I gained a great boss and real good friend-
Sometimes The Lords favor is hard to swallow,
But when you do what's right, blessings will follow.

So if you're down, please don't give up,
And never refer to God's blessings as good luck-
But give Him praise for what He's done,
For those who believe, redemption will come!

"A job from Jesus."

Sink Or Swim

To keep from going under,
You must learn to swim-
Sometimes life makes you wonder,
While holding on to a broken limb.

Retreat doesn't always mean defeat,
When there are no options left-
Sometimes life can be bittersweet,
How long can you hold your breath.

For me the edge was out of reach,
And no one threw a rope-
No one listened when I tried to teach,
That's when I lost all hope.

The beginning justifies the end,
In spite of how you go-
Now I don't have to pretend,
You only saw what I wanted to show.

"When the pain becomes too unbearable from the vicissitudes of life, we need others to become our wind and carry us."

Set Adrift   **60.**

Set adrift on a memory bliss,
At the tender age of 46.
I cried so hard in my back yard-
And my head I couldn't lift.

Prince Be, you inspired me,
And will be sorely missed.
I'm truly sorry you're gone-
R.I.P. to Attrell Cordes of P.M. Dawn.

"Gone 2 soon."

Self-Reflection (A Look Inside)   **61.**

I took a look inside to self-reflect,
To determine which version deserved respect.
I had to decide who I wanted to be,
The version I create myself, or the one passed down to me.
I discovered the truth by continuing to persist,
Having the power to choose is a noble gift.
I choose to become the best I can be,
And receive the blessings that God has for me.

"Search your soul and find (re-define) your true self."

Serenity (A Peaceful Place Within Yourself)

I meditate-
My soul finds refuge in a peaceful state.
I open my mind to discover more of me-
I close my eyes to see.

Human beings are complex.
We change,
We grow-
We evolve,
From one context to the next.

Thoughts don't remain the same with an evolving brain-
So refrain from thinking as such.
Maturation is the process for the soul to develop-
And to grow up.

So be at peace with yourself if you want to be free-
This is the true state of serenity.

"He will keep you in perfect peace whose mind is
stayed on Him."
Isaiah 26:3

10 Timely Truths

1). False expectations leads to loss of elevation.
2). Expect more of yourself than anyone else.
3). Carry hope in your own bag.
4). Live your passion and make your soul glad.
5). Frowns weigh more.
6). So wear a smile before you walk out the door.
7). Don't feed into negativity or you'll consume too much.
8). Get in tune with yourself and never give up.
9). God is the source where love and life begin.
10). Seek His face and flee from sin.

10 Spiritual Truths

Feelings, *provoke thoughts.*

Thoughts, *promote words.*

Words, *provide hope.*

Hope, *generates faith.*

Faith, *inspires joy.*

Joy, *creates goodness.*

Goodness, *expresses love.*

Love, *gives life.*

Life, *reveals God.*

God *encompasses all.*

The Poetic Flame   64.
For my brother Fred

You didn't have a lot,
But gave what you had-
I was blessed from what I got,
And left uplifted and glad.

When I struggled you were always there,
A true friend in times of need-
You showed up because you cared,
Because of your example I follow your lead.

Watching you write your Easter Piece,
Inspired me to do the same-
Because of you my gift is released,
You ignited in me the poetic flame.

My success is from seeds you've sown,
Thank you for having me in your view-
Wherever I go your name will be known,
Truly honored having a brother like you.

"Eternally grateful for having you as a brother. Thank you so much Fred for laying the poetic foundation."

The Poetic Zone   **65.**

When I'm alone-
I go into a mode known as the poetic zone.

Then poetic messages flow across my mind like water-
And drip into my subconscious.

And as I become conscious-
I drink, and they become my own.

"Creativity takes place when I'm alone in the zone."

The Eagles Plight 66.

When eagles die,
It's a sad day-
For they fly high,
To show us the way.

Soaring in the wind,
Then spiraling to the ground-
Because untamed men,
Shoot them down.

"Eagles are majestic birds and they inspire us to reach new heights.
When they are no more, mankind will soon follow."

The Same Sun And Moon

The same sun shined long ago,
As men toiled under its rays-
But it won't shine for much longer,
Because we're living in the last days-
In case you didn't know.

The same moon shined too,
As men looked upon the midnight sky-
They pondered about the hereafter,
And where the soul goes after you die-
Because we're just passing through.

The same sun provided inspiration,
And shines as a beacon of hope-
Some quit dreaming when the sun goes down,
While alone in the dark they grope-
Then commit acts of desperation.

Now is your T.I.M.E under the sun,
You won't get another chance to re-do-
So get busy before your T.I.M.E is up,
T.I.M.E is a curfew to help you stay true-
So leave no work undone.

"The sun and moon remain the same. What needs to change is me and you."

The Truth Revealed   68.

The truth was concealed,
But now is revealed-
The rock was rolled away,
Because He arose that day.

"I Am the resurrection and the life."
John 11:25

The Bread Of Life   69.

Oh taste and see that The Lord is sweet,
But take heed to God's promise of death-
Of every tree you are free to eat,
Except the one that takes your last breath.

It's easy for men to fall into sin,
That's why we plead the blood of Christ-
As disciples, we need to be more like Him,
The one who is the Bread of Life.

But the sting of death won't last forever,
Death is a tool for God's divine plan-
When life won't suffice death brings us together,
He has the whole world in His hands.

Oh taste and see that The Lord is sweet,
But don't allow sin to lead you astray-
Wells containing the river of life run deep,
For His glory we are vessels made of clay.

"I am the bread of life."
John 6:35

The Second Verse

Life is more than the first sentence,
So have hope in the second verse-
A change of direction is true repentance,
Your life is blessed and was never cursed.

Enemies come to steal, kill and destroy,
And won't stop until they see you defeated-
They prey on innocent girls and boys,
But God's work in you hasn't been completed.

The devil is no respect of persons,
On earth he's launched a vicious attack-
We all need God's protection that's for certain,
Regardless if you're white or black.

Trust in God's plan for you,
You're a star that was designed to shine-
Give Him praise in all that you do,
Complete healing is a matter of time.

"I know the plans I have for you."
Jeremiah 29:11

The Earth Remains

Many will come to believe,
As false prophets continue to deceive-
Blaspheming His name while living in vain,
But the earth remains.

The simple ones are easily seduced,
Led astray from rejecting the truth-
Then succumb from the cost of fame,
But the earth remains.

The wicked will fall by the sword,
Hearing the gospel they laughed and ignored-
And sold their soul for material gain,
But the earth remains.

But for believers who receive the light,
They are precious in the Father's sight-
Blood washed from sins crimson stain,
But the earth remains.

> Generations come and go, but the earth remains forever."
> Ecclesiastes 1:4

The Matrix   72.

All that openeth the matrix is mine,
And every firstling among thy cattle-
The first born of the womb is divine,
Consecrated for the day of battle.

The One has come to show the way,
For those who veered off the chosen path-
To their shame they have gone astray,
But when the wicked fall, I will laugh.

The One will soon make His return,
Armageddon is war between good and evil-
Calamities will come and the earth will burn,
But those called by My name will be My people.

Behold, I make all things new,
The former things have passed away-
Ancient prophecies were trustworthy and true,
The faithful enjoy Heaven on earth each day.

"For behold I return quickly."
Revelation 22:12

Today   73.

Today is a new day,
So make it a good one-
Have edifying words to say,
And go have some fun.

Share your love and light,
Try things you never did-
Strive to do what's right,
Kiss and hug your kids.

Stop and lend a hand,
To your neighbor in need-
Do the best you can,
You're known by your deeds.

Make tomorrow jealous of today,
End today on a positive note-
Before bed don't forget to pray,
And you'll wake up with hope.

Tomorrow

Tomorrow is not promised to you,
You may transition today-
If you don't think this is true,
Remember those who passed away.

"Yesterday was a gift that you might not receive tomorrow."

The Power Of Love   74.

The power of love,
Is my kind of power-
That comes from above,
This is our darkest hour.

We all need introspect,
On how we treat each other-
The key is mutual respect,
Working together as brothers.

There's fear on both sides,
How did we come to this-
Division will be our demise,
Hate must cease and desist.

Healing needs to take place,
For crimes against humanity-
God's love transcends race,
Only the truth will set us free.

"The only power that can save us is the power of love."

The Procrastinator

Unsown seeds never got planted-
Because **The Procrastinator** took his seeds for granted.

He never sowed his seeds,
Thinking they would be choked by the weeds-
And he reaped what he believed.

"But cast your bread upon the waters and ye shall reap a harvest after many days."
Ecclesiastes 11:1.

The Limelight   76.

Here's the deal-
The limelight kills.
It leads to costly thrills-
Risk taking, drugs, alcohol and popping pills.
There are other means to pay your bills-
Be healed, get sober and cleave to what's real.

"Not everyone who's in the "limelight" engages in (or succumbs to) negative behaviors. This piece is not intended to imply that everyone who's in the public eye engages in such behavior. **This piece is merely a reflection on those beautiful souls who have succumbed (and ultimately had unresolved issues of the heart).** Oftentimes when negative behaviors are exhibited there are deeper unresolved issues at work. And the limelight seemingly fosters a culture to self-medicate from those issues."

The Cross   77.

Don't lose sight of the cross,
But in case you get lost-
It will be a saving light,
And guide you through the night.

"The cross is where Christ made atonement for sin and where new life begins."

The Reckoning 78.

I asked myself, why am I here,
At home I wasn't the man any more-
I knew my departure was drawing near,
So I packed my bags and walked out the door.

I jumped in my truck and headed south,
But didn't know where I would end up-
Rumors abound from people running their mouths,
But people need to keep their mouths shut.

Sometimes what you need is a new start,
To see new things and reinvent yourself-
It hurts, but you try not to fall apart,
And pride says you don't need anyone else.

Only God knows what lies ahead,
But I'll give it all that I got-
I'll return to Springfield when I'm old and dead,
Why stay where you're not wanted and rot.

"When you've outlived your welcome it's time for change."

Thick Skin

I once had thick skin,
Like bark on a tree-
But now it's thin,
From her words to me.

Poisonous words cut,
Like the sharpest knife-
Or punch to the gut,
Venom spewed from strife.

Why would you say that,
To someone you love-
And can't take it back,
Spite is not from above.

Words contain power,
I feel broken inside-
Like a wilted flower,
A part of me died.

"The tongue is a restless evil full of deadly poison."
James 3:8

Trapped _____ 80.

I'm trapped inside but I wanna be free,
But how do I know if it's meant to be-
Blindly I trust what you are saying to me,
If freedom is sweet, I must taste and see!

"Many of our ancestors died chasing freedom. So live a life worthy of their sacrifices."

Thug Life To Superman

The devil put me to the test,
Inside my mind there was no rest-
I was living in sin I must confess,
Thug Life ain't nothing but a mess.

Shooting guns like the wild wild west,
I was gang-banging trying to impress-
And I always wore a bullet proof vest,
Mad at the world and couldn't care less.

The shame from sin had me depressed,
My spirit was broken from all the stress-
So I started searching for a new quest,
And when I cried out The Lord blessed.

The life I once lived I now digress,
Now I pack my Bible whenever I dress-
And daily I give The Lord my best,
To reflect the S that's on my chest.

"There's a superman inside us all. Change and discover him."

The Grind, Competition And Success   82.

The competition keeps me on my grind.
But to reach new heights-
Old habits must stay behind.

I'll reach my destiny by staying true to me,
I'm striving to become the best I can be.

Don't let past failure equal current defeat,
There's just a deeper level that God wants you to reach.

Obstacles will put your faith to the test,
But hard work and perseverance is the recipe for success.

And pay no mind to the critics on the sideline.
Just stay on your grind-
And the competition you'll always outshine.

"Are you in the game making it happen or just a critic on the sideline?"

The Answer Is Me
For Allen Iverson

I came into the league in '96
When California Love was the hottest remix-
Some say the greatest athlete since Muhammad Ali,
The game is the question but the answer is me.

I scored and then stepped over Tyronn Lue,
Guarding me was a task he could not do-
Then I shook Mike at the top of the key,
The game is the question but the answer is me.

Playing with heart led to the hall of fame,
Now all future ballers will remember my name-
Driven to become the best I could be,
The game is the question but the answer is me.

Playing in the league was a labor of love,
My skills were a gift from God above-
There are no limits to what anyone can be,
The game is the question but the answer is me.

"You played each game like it was your last. Thank you A. I. for the memories. Pound for pound you're the greatest of all time."

The Right Voice   **84.**

You won't get far selling this book,
A complete stranger said this to me-
You'd be better off being a crook,
I turned and said, "**Just wait and see!**"

It hurts when people don't believe in you,
People discourage you because it's not them-
But keep doing what you're supposed to do,
Hating on me because his outlook is dim.

Never lose hope from what others say,
What God has for you will come to pass-
Keep believing in yourself and always pray,
What comes from The Lord will always last.

If I believed his words I wouldn't be here,
Success In Life Is A Personal Choice-
Everyone doesn't deserve your listening ear,
So make sure you're listening to the right voice.

"Stay true to you."

What's The Point?   85.

What's the point of doing good,
When you only report my bad-
I didn't always do what I should,
But when I failed, why were you glad.

Hypocrites and backstabbers is all I see,
But why critique me before looking at yourself-
What legitimate ought do you have against me,
Your mirror wasn't intended for somebody else.

Haters spread rumors and outright lies,
Because they have nothing better to do-
They have a fault finding spirit and critical eyes,
Under the sun there is nothing new.

Hateful people thrive off negativity,
Love for others is not in their DNA-
But negative press won't get the best of me,
Because what they sow, karma sends their way.

"When others try to confine you to your past it's
because that's where they're at.
Just leave them there and keep moving in a positive
direction."

Why I Left — 86.

I tried to hang in there and do what's right-
But you get tired of all the fussing every night.

My kids deserve better from her and me-
A dysfunctional home they don't need to see.

I need to breathe that's why I chose to leave-
Why stay when the love is gone and grieve?

"When love has left the building it's time to move on and rebuild."

When Poets Cry

When Prince died I was in Nashville driving a semi-
Overwhelmed by sadness, I pulled over and cried.

What Is God To Me?

God to me is talent I see-
And is daily expressed.
Great ones, from Prince to Muhammad Ali-
Who blessed the world by giving their best.

"The Genius and The Champ has passed and my heart still remains sad. There will never be another like them. Thank you Prince for your musical contribution and thank you Champ for your courageous stand. R.I.P. to both."

Work While It's Day   88.

The time has come for us to pray,
Many won't live to see another day.
To our graves one day we all must go,
Some arrive fast, while others tarry slow.

Death comes to all under the sun,
Youth isn't proof that old age will come.
As night becomes day with the rising of the sun,
So work while its day for night is sure to come.

"Work while its day for when night cometh,
no man shall work."
John 9:4

When Your Story Ends 89.

No one cared when he was alive,
Until he was found hanging from a tree-
The tears he cried were hidden inside,
From an internal struggle you could not see.

There were too many costly temptations,
For him to resist every fleshly desire-
He was suicidal from demonic provocation,
His final goodbye before baptism by fire.

Who knows where the spirit of man goes,
Whether back to his Creator or down below-
Only God and His son Jesus Christ know,
But when your story ends it's time to go.

Lesson 1. *Learn the meaning of true love-*
Lesson 2. *Have the courage to care,*
Lesson 3. *Remember, there's only one judge,*
Lesson 4. *Show kindness and share.*

"A man who had silent tears and hidden fears and who was looking for a listening ear."

Why? 90.

Why is it hard to live, but easy to die?
Why is it hard to be honest, but easy to lie?
Why is it easy to lose, but hard to win?
Why is it easy to quit, but hard to begin?

Why is it hard to stay afloat, but easy to sink?
Why is it hard to stay sober, but easy to drink?
Why is it hard to save, but easy to go broke?
Why is it hard to keep the faith, but easy to lose hope?

"The struggle is real but so are the answers. Tell the truth and keep it simple."

Who's Coming Behind You?

What can a man do who succeeds the king?
But pick up where he left off and fulfill his dream-
But coming behind me won't be easy to do,
Because I'm motivated from what I've been through.

"Who is your successor?"

Wisdom   92.

A man's wisdom makes his face shine,
And the reason why I wear a smile-
Before birth I was commissioned by the divine,
And rescued while floating down the Nile.

A wise man discerns both time and judgment,
Man's deceitful heart is cause to be alarmed-
Studying God's Word is time well spent,
Any snake might bite when not being charmed.

Wisdom spoken quietly should always be heard,
There are no sounds coming from the grave-
But when fools hear wisdom it sounds absurd,
Without wisdom you're only fit for being a slave.

Thy wisdom have I hidden in my heart,
Man was made upright with lessons to learn-
When trials come, those without wisdom fall apart,
For dust we are, and to dust we shall return.

"Wisdom is the principle thing. Therefore, get wisdom."
Proverbs 4:7

Wordplay

Don't be quick to give your words away,
Every thought you don't have to say-
Your issues prevent you from writing today,
But deliverance comes when you pray.

Put the pipe down and pick the pen back up,
And think outside the box when you're stuck-
Will others continue to care if you don't give a _____?
The smallest volcano will eventually erupt.

Taming one's tongue seems an impossible task,
But a soft answer turns away wrath-
Questions are more likely answered when respectfully asked,
Time equals money, now you do the math.

Words are like birds they have wings and fly,
Words live on in people's hearts after you die,
Words can't be taken back no matter how hard you try,
Words can turn deadly after they make you cry.

"May the words of my mouth and thoughts in my heart
be acceptable in your sight."
Psalms 19:14

Wait'n On Money 94.

I got some money coming my way,
But it ain't coming fast enough-
To survive, I need it to arrive today,
Because my riverbank has dried up.

Steady flow really means a lot,
Especially when you've made plans-
But pockets full of lent is all I got,
When you're broke, you feel less than a man.

When I had money I should've saved more,
Dying of thirst staring down an empty well-
With the demon of poverty I am at war,
Money is akin to heaven and being broke is hell!

Alas, my money has finally arrived,
It took a while but I'm glad it's here-
In the desert suffering and I almost died,
Now money is flowing and I drink without fear.

"Money is the answer for all things."
Ecclesiastes 10:19

When I Go

When I die how will I go,
Inquiring minds want to know-
But I'll go the way the righteous do,
The way I choose too.

Who among you can predict their demise,
Only those with insight beyond the skies-
Like Jesus "The Messiah" who knew His time,
I, "Da Moody Poet" also know mine.

It's nothing short of a mental burden,
That's because I know for certain-
Don't ask and God won't tell,
But Heaven awaits, I've already been thru hell.

In the 11th hour the pen will drop,
On the 8th day the poetry will stop-
Fret not because it won't be the end,
3 days later I'll be writing again.

"My Premonition."

Walking In My Destiny   96.

Come and see me for what,
What will I be looking at-
Someone who's given up,
Opposites don't always attract.

But why come and see me,
And not have good news-
I'm alone but not lonely,
You won't ruin my groove.

I have come too far,
To take a setback now-
I'm shining like a star,
And staying true to my vow.

I'm striving to be great,
No more drama for me-
I'm blessed for His name sake,
And walking in my destiny!

"Refuse to be victimized. Cut unhealthy ties.
Don't believe the devils lies.
Keep your eyes upon the prize and you will self-actualize."

What Color Is Your Water?

(A conversation between a 12 year old African American girl from Flint and a peer from Grosse Pointe. Witnessed by her father who chronicled the conversation).

What color is your water?
A question posed to my 12 year old daughter,
My water is the color of my skin-
Because of the community I live in.

But in Grosse Pointe your water is crystal clear,
I'm sad because it's not that way around here-
But instead our water is poisoned with lead,
And I'm afraid I'll get sick or end up dead.

I go to bed scared and suffer from nightmares,
And these racist politicians don't even care-
They told us our water was safe to drink,
While harmful toxins were flowing through our sink.

We need new pipes and a fresh water supply,
Because we're poor and black, they told us a lie-
This is totally unacceptable to the children of Flint,
We deserve better from where our childhood is spent.

"Clean Water Matters!"

Your Cross

When no one else is there,
Take it to The Lord in prayer-
It hurts when people don't care,
But this cross is too heavy to bear.

Prayer and faith will see you through,
Trusting God is what you now must do-
Perfect peace is what He's offering to you,
The promises of God will always come true.

This storm is a temporary trial,
That will only last a little while-
It takes courage to quit living in denial,
Grace awaits as you walk down that isle.

God's open arms are ready to receive,
All He requires is for you to believe-
Rejecting His love makes His heart grieve,
God seeks those who are lost and deceived.

**"Cast your cares upon Him for He cares for you."
1 Peter 5:7**

Yesterday
For Tara. Thank you.

Yesterday I almost gave up,
Because life can be a hard hustle-
Sometimes life can truly suck,
And you have to flex your muscle.

Yesterday felt like a day from hell,
Because I had a real close call-
I almost stayed down after I fell,
Thankfully, I'm back standing tall.

Yesterday I started to lose hope,
Everywhere I turned there was someone cruel-
Life to me was becoming a joke,
You get tired of playing the fool.

Yesterday is now behind me,
I thank God for a new day-
I'm making a choice to be happy,
And nothing will take my joy away.

"Don't allow today's pain, problems or sorrow to carry over into tomorrow."

Your Success   100.

When dreams end you must wake-up doing,
Set reachable goals and then start pursuing-
Take calculated steps in a positive direction,
The Lord will guide you and be your protection

Waiting on tomorrow could be a costly mistake,
T.I.M.E. is limited so don't wait too late-
Obstacles along the way are only a test,
For your success what are you willing to invest?

The Father breathed His Spirit into you,
Through His son, there's nothing you can't do-
But without faith nothing will come to pass,
Dreams deferred shatter like broken glass.

You were created to let your light shine,
But you can't lead if you're left behind-
What you have to offer other's clearly see,
So aspire to become all that you can be.

"Greatness lies within you!"

Zealot   101.

He came to convict the world of sin-
And died on the cross as the savior of men.

Three days later He rose from the grave-
And the path to Heaven was officially paved.

"I Am the way and the truth and the life, no man comes
to the Father except through me."
John 14:6

Bonus Poems

The Proliferation Of Mass Communication   X.

Nowadays there's no real contact-
Only a tweet back.

In times past we didn't need the internet to reconnect-
Back then we had real friends, real love and mutual respect.

But today it's not like that-
Now we got Facebook, Periscope, Email, Instagram and Snapchat.

Communication these days ain't what it used to be-
Because now all we do is say, *just text me.*

> "Let's get back to real community and real communication."

<u>Give and Create</u>   XX.

Let us give and create to change our own fate.
Not having that level of clout is what the rage is all about-
And no faith in the justice system breed's fear and doubt.
Look at Milwaukee's segregation and their prison population-
Only serious legislation will diffuse acts of desperation.
When things are actually as they seem-
It's easy to lose hope in the *"American Dream."*
Now imagine the shoe on the other foot-
You shouldn't victim blame when inequality is the root.
But at the same time, we are running out of time-
Because now things have gotten way out of line.
Since those in power choose to stay blind,
Let us give and create to change our own fate-
Or soon it will be too late.

"Peace to all our communities.

Especially: Flint, Ferguson, Milwaukee, Chicago, Tulsa, California and Charlotte."

Odyssey (Christ's Journey To Manhood)   XXX.

In a manger I arrived,
And born for a great destiny-
But the goal is to stay alive,
God's Angels will protect me.

I will feed off truth,
And grow big and strong-
Within me lies righteous roots,
But will be falsely accused of doing wrong.

My zeal is to do His will,
To set the captives free-
In me salvation is revealed,
To Heaven's Gate I hold the key.

My Father will never forsake me,
I came to fulfill His plan-
To reconcile God with humanity,
Then I'll return home a man.

"For to us a child is born. To us a son is given."
Isaiah 9:6

The Long Walk Home   XXXX.
(A 12-year-old future Nina Simone)

It was a long walk home-
But the moon followed, so I wasn't alone.
Into the night I aimlessly roamed-
But I'm destined to be great, like Nina Simone.

She was beautiful like me-
Adorned with African attributes.
But concerned about incessant trees-
That was hanging strange fruit.

At school I was an outcast,
And it bothered me some-
Made to sit at the back of the class,
As peers jeered and made fun.

While in back I imagined being up front,
To be loved and accepted is what every child wants.

But I'm proud like Nina Simone was-
Because black is beautiful and the color of love.

So I studied hard to prove my self-worth-
Knowing I descend from Nubian Queens of the earth.

But on my long walk home I began to cry,
From thoughts of rejection beneath the moonlit sky.

But daddy hugged me and wiped my tears away,
And like Langston, I Too will grow strong each day.

I'll be a woman of valor when full grown-
And leave a legacy of greatness like Nina Simone.

The Poetic Call

"It is an artist duty to reflect the times in which we live."
-Nina Simone

Poets are thinkers and dreamers,
We are the nation's thermostat-
We pray for every negative schemer,
Expressing where their level of pain is at.

Poets remain on the front lines,
Fighting to change unjust situations-
Speaking truth to power is our only crime,
Preventing the further decline of our nation.

Poetic gifts are given to share,
Through rhythmic verse or melodic song-
Inspiring those entrusted to our care,
Promoting the mutual need to get along.

Poets see beyond and go deeper,
Poets seek to heal and promote unity-
Poets are love warriors and truth seekers,
Poets transmit hope throughout their community.

"Will You Answer The Call?"

Thank you for your interest in Miscellaneous Pieces.
I hope you enjoyed.
Peace and God Bless!

All poems and quotes in this book were written and arranged by Robert L. Horton and are copyright protected.
For questions or comments about his book,
please contact Robert at: Preshome4education@yahoo.com or damoodypoet@gmail.com